eds
ht?

e in
y:

meet
can
t.

and
se.
for

Harry's Home!

A Cat Compendium

By Susan Jane Smith
with stories from Janet Arnold, Christine Warwick and Rose Giles

Harry's Home! A Cat Compendium

© Copyright 2006 Susan Jane Smith

Published and distributed by Counselling in the Forest, Copse Edge, Lower Road, Yorkley, Lydney, Gloucestershire, England GL15 4TN
Tel: 01594 564308 or email susanjane.smith@btconnect.com.

1st printing September 2006
Printed in England

ISBN 0-9553698-1-9
    978-0-9553698-1-0

**£1 from each purchase will go to support cat rescue work.
See the promise to Sooty!**

www.harryishome.co.uk

Dedication

to
Carol Claxton
Photographer Extraordinaire

of

Harry

and
for
her
support,
fun and laughter!

Acknowledgements

Harry's "Aunties" (Janet Arnold, Christine Warwick, and Rose Giles) deserve my thanks. They have been brave enough to share stories for public critique and, hopefully, enjoyment. They are all devoted cat lovers, needless to say!

Appreciation also goes to my Husband, Richard, for proof reading with patience!

Last, but not least, a big *"thank you"* to "Auntie Carol" for her patience in photographing the "Young Prince" (as Harry has now been called by Auntie Christine!).

Contents

Harry's Introduction

My Mum fancies herself as Mrs. Doolittle (like the Doctor who could talk to the animals)! She hasn't quite made the grade yet!

She has always been besotted with cats! Here she is aged 2! Grandfather's cat was just too tempting!

Mum says she likes the naïve quality of these photos because they are just simple snaps that people have taken. If you want sophisticated this is not the book for you!

Mum also says that since she has "road tested" the book on "Auntie" Carol (my photographer) the book may make you sad in places but it will also give you lots of chuckles!

I am just the latest in a long life of feline friends!

Here's my Mum as a little girl with one of her cats…name long forgotten!

The love these felines have given and received will be familiar to cat lovers the world over. There's nothing new or different here – just simple stories about the cats who've shared my Mum's life. She has got lots of cat stories. A couple of friends have shared stories too. I have lots of "Aunties"!

These are all true stories even though some of them are hard to believe.

I hope you enjoy these tales as all cats create pure bliss, says Mum.
She thinks she can earn some cat food through sharing them with you.
I hope you like this book as I love my tummy!

Mum says that some of the money will go to keep her promise to Sooty
so do read on to find out all about him!

Puss: The Story of a Very Brave Boy

This is a story of love and courage and trust.
It has a happy ending. Three legs are enough!

I met a woman called Jean the other day who told me her story of amazing devotion - not just on her part but on the part of her cat, Puss. We had started talking because of my three legged cat, Holly. Puss must have had enormous trust in this lady. Puss had gone out for his normal walk and got caught in a trap! These are illegal. Still some people put them out – frequently farmers - so beware if you live near fields!

Now Jean didn't know this. He just went missing. She and her family looked and looked for him, as you do. In her heart Jean knew that something bad must have happened because he always came home. She knew that if he hadn't come home it meant he couldn't get home.

Eight days went by and she'd almost given up hope. Then when she came home that evening she heard a very faint meow. It was coming from Puss's favourite spot. Hope rose. It crashed down again when she got there.

Puss was home, but in an awful condition. The lower part of his leg was missing and the rest of the leg was gangrenous. There were even maggots to be seen coming from the wounds. She wrapped him up and rushed off to the Vets. They thought the kindest thing would be to put him to sleep. In order to get himself free, the Vet said he had chewed his own leg off. The pain must have been extraordinary. Many another would have died just from the shock and trauma.

Jean figured that if he trusted her enough to drag himself home to her the least she could do was to give him every chance medical science and love could offer. She did not let him down.

The vets removed his leg right up at the joint where it joined his body. That was after a very anxious 24 hours on a drip to try to improve his dehydration, etc. Jean was told very firmly that the risk was high, that he probably would not make it. He did.

Lots of TLC (tender loving care) and home with the humans he loved, he has a learned to manage on 3 legs and is happy again! I like happy endings.

There is nothing like a cuddle with your best friend!

My First Kittens and the Two Greys

I was about five years old and living in the U.S.A. when this litter was born. There are no photos of the mother cat and nor do I remember her. I cannot remember a time when a cat was not in my life as we always had cats and so did all my Grandparents and other relatives.

I just remember playing with these little ones…all young creatures together. This was at a time when I also had a pet black hen that followed me around and there was a dog, and ducks too!

I was about nine when two grey kittens were acquired from across the road. I don't remember what happened to the previous lot of cats, and sadly my parents are now dead so I have no one to ask.

What I remember is that these two grey kittens were a brother and sister and the first kittens I got to choose! The man across the road had a whole litter! I don't remember their names. What I very clearly remember is dressing the boy up in my dolls clothes. He would lie on his back in my dolls pram with a dolls baby bottle of milk between his paws – I don't suppose he actually got any milk out though! I remember as it was my favourite "party trick"! I always got admiration from my Mum because she never got over the fact that he let me do it! I loved him wholeheartedly and I'd like to think I didn't do him any harm! I know not what happened to them as I was dragged off to England for one of my Mum's protracted visits and they must have been given away.

The greys were still there, though, when I was given two baby turkey chicks for Easter. In The States there is a tradition of having a white (bunny) rabbit for Easter and that was what I normally had (I think they actually ended up in the stew pot as they were never around the following Easter). I have been a vegetarian for years because I cannot bear the thought of eating an animal!

Anyway these two chicks initially lived in a cardboard box by the side of my bed and slept with me and the grey cats. The turkeys got quite big before "disappearing". I'd love to know what the cats thought of sharing life with growing turkeys!

The Six He Killed

Somewhere in between the first kittens and the grey ones there was another cat which had a litter of six kittens. They were battered to death by the little boy next door. He was only four at the time.

It still horrifies me today. Every summer when I was a child growing up in New Hampshire, U.S.A. we spent the time at the lake. We went to our large static caravan right down by the water. It was in a trailer park on Lake Winnipesauke near Laconia. They were sumptuous summers – I played all day in the sand and swam in the lake from dawn to dusk. It was safe to just let your children play out. I had lots of friends. Life was so simple and innocent then…

I was about 8 and we had been into town in Dad's car for shopping. My friends were waiting at the top of the very long dirt track when we turned in, which was unusual. They ran up to the car crying and pointing and shouting all at once so I never really understood what was said.

I can still see them now and I can still feel the pain even though that was almost fifty years ago. I lost my innocence about the world being a lovely place that day. When we got to our caravan I was ushered straight inside. Mum tried to explain it to me, but I don't think I really took it in because I had never come across death before. I just remember crying as if my heart would break.

Apparently my parents had left my kittens in a cardboard box with the mother cat under the trailer because they would be cooler there whilst we went shopping. The little boy from next door had taken a piece of wood and had hit them all till they were dead (the mother cat had fled). What is worse to me, is that my friends saw him and ran to tell his mother. She was drinking and laughing with people at a neighbouring trailer and wouldn't budge. She was less than 10 feet away and did nothing to stop this mayhem. She did not even bother to go and look.

All these years later with my training as a Psychotherapist, I can see that the little boy was probably a victim himself or had witnessed other terrible scenes and was just acting them out. Understanding that does not ease the pain. My heartache today is for the fear and pain my kittens must have suffered before death.

He must have been at it quite a while. It has instilled in me a strong desire to protect the weak and vulnerable. They had been just little balls of fluff – not even eight weeks old!

I have often wondered what kind of a man that boy grew up to become.

Pudding

She was a brown tabby kitten – fat as a butter ball and I was "home for Christmas" staying at my Auntie Jane's near Chepstow. Just one of many farm kittens was Pudding, but allowed inside for some reason. She looked like a Christmas pudding and thus her name. My love of her started when I was crying over splitting up with yet another chap (I was in my twenties, divorced by my choice, but not choosing men wisely).

Pudding came along the back of the settee and licked my tears away. I was so very touched at the time. Cynics may well be saying it was the salt she was after!

Anyway, back to my flat in Milton Keynes she came and in due course I thought she should go to the Vet to be "fixed". She screamed all the way there. And I do mean screamed. I didn't believe in telepathy at the time. I just felt I should not be doing this, but I could find no logical reason not to go ahead.

The Vet was a very tall man with huge hands and very gentle as he lifted her out of her box. She looked so tiny in those hands. He called me later that day and cried as he told me her heart had given out on the operating table. This was back in 1974 so I expect veterinary medicine has moved on from then. He said he'd even given her mouth to mouth resuscitation. I was very touched at the thought of that big man trying to save that little kitten.

Tiffy, Darling and the Stretch Limo!

Tiffy and Darling were my cats in the U.S.A. and when I decided to return to England in 1989 I couldn't leave them behind. It cost me all the profit from the sale of my house to get us all to the U.K. – two dogs included of course!

Anyway, British Airways was very helpful and after lots of international telephone calls I arranged their stay in a quarantine cattery and kennels in Buckinghamshire. I did all the paperwork and the only problem left was getting us to the airport an hour away from where I lived! It was August and over 90 degrees Fahrenheit. The only transportation I could find that had air conditioning was a stretch limousine! We travelled in style that day and I don't think the driver will ever forget it. He was more used to taking brides to church in his beautiful, leather upholstered, white car! I crammed the cat and dog boxes in along with my luggage on the back seat and off we went. They had already been sedated and boxed to meet regulations. It's the only time I've ever been in a limo! I don't expect too many other animals have done so since! Pets of celebrities excluded of course!

This is Tiffy and Darling in the quarantine cattery – very cosy!

Tina and Tessa

This is Tessa in later years.

Tessa came into my life after my Mother's death. Originally Mum had wanted a pair of kittens and so Tina and Tessa, who were out of the same litter and looked almost identical (except Tina had green eyes and Tessa orange ones), went to Mum. She was wheelchair bound and soon found that whilst Tessa was happy to ride on her lap, Tina thought running through the wheels of the moving chair great fun! Too much stress for Mum so Tina moved in with me. Tessa stayed with Mum until her death.

Tessa was with my Mother's body all night long on the night she died, and when I got there the next morning she was terribly distressed. After finishing with the police, medics and all that happens with an unexpected death, I took Tessa home with me. I popped her straight into the spare bedroom and she literally bounced off the walls. After a fortnight of this I had almost given up hope of her being able to stay, but then suddenly, all by herself, she settled.

Tessa has slept with me every night since, so that's about 17 years of the comforting sound of purring in my ear to send me off to dream land. I find purring such a comfort. That's also how I usually wake up – to the sound of Tessa purring. Such a privilege. She is very special as she is my last link to my Mother and will be sorely missed one day. Now she is still feisty!

What she made me think about is that I have lived my 56 years with the soothing sound of purrs – how lucky I've been! Cats have played such a large part in my life – they have listened to all my woes and joy and never criticised! I truly believe it is our privilege to share our life with a cat – and preferably more than one!

The Adventures of Tessa the Kitten

A STORY FOR CHILDREN
TRUE JUST LIKE THE OTHERS!

"One fine, sunny February day five cats went out to play. There was Sugar, the big black Persian tom cat, all fluffy with white bib and paws and a high silver ruff. There was Darling, the elderly one, all white with palest grey and beige patches. She was 16 so very old and not interested in venturing far from the kitchen and food.

Then there was Beauty, a chocolate box cat, all fluffy and tabby with a great desire to catch the birds at the feeder in the garden. Tina was the tiniest and had been the runt of the litter. She was almost identical to Tessa, just a bit smaller and rounder.

And then there was Tessa. She was the hunter/explorer who would go, along the brook, to follow its path and see all that she could see. She would run out of the back door of the cottage, over the bridge to the garden at the back (where two brooks met) over the old tree stump, and then along the edge of the field, and away she went. Her human mother could not follow her through the bushes, and had to wait for her return. Up the path, that she had made, by the babbling brook, she went. Up the field to where the rabbits played. Tessa was a ginger tortie and had a white bib and so from a distance, she looked like a fox.

At first, the rabbits were scared of her. Other cats had come and taken their babies away to eat. After four visits and lots of sniffs, they decided to trust what Tessa "said"– she just wanted to play and see what rabbit life was like. The more often she went to visit, the more the rabbits believed she meant them no harm. She'd just sit and watch them as they played.

So, on this special day, they let her join in. Oh, what fun they had. They ran and chased each other in a game of tag, up hill and down and round and round. The sun shone and they played so hard they forgot the time.

Tessa could hear her Mummy calling so she said "goodbye" to her new friends, promised she'd come back as soon as she could and scampered home.

The big black crow, which lived in the hedge, flew up and called out angrily as she passed by. She had run so fast and so quietly that he'd not heard her coming, so he got a bit of a fright! Still it told her Mum where she was and that she was coming in for her meal at last!

Tessa ran all the way home, jumped into her Mum's arms for lots of kisses and cuddles and had a bit of food. As Tessa and the other four cats snuggled down on their Mummy's bed, she had a wonderful story to tell of her adventures in the village of Beachampton and off to sleep they all went."

The Courthouse Cats

![image](the courthouse cats photo)

These are just a few!

In 1998 I was a Family Mediator and Professional Practice Consultant for the Family Mediators Association and the U. K. College of Family Mediation and I was granted a government contract for mediation - financed by the Legal Aid Board. This meant that I had to find "proper" office space rather than working from home. The Old Courthouse in Fenny Stratford, Milton Keynes was newly renovated and so seemed a great place to go. I moved into a suite of offices there and at the end of the first day, I went out to my car to go home. What did I find but a very poorly, ancient cat sat by my car. Why me?

He was the scruffiest old cat I've ever seen. He was black and white and ancient and dusty and oh so thin. I brought him a dish of food the next morning and fed him under my car to try to keep him safe in such a busy car park! Heartbreaking, but I couldn't touch him as he was too nervous and I simply did not know what else to do for him then.

Well, you might be able to guess what happened next! That night there were a couple of other poor scraps of cats by my car and on it went until I was feeding what turned out to be a feral colony of 13! They recognised a soft touch! It got too much for the car park and I started feeding them down on a rough patch of ground at the end of the car park which was nettle infested but of course I cleared them!

I went around to the other women in the building and we all brought food in for them. They were very skittish, but so glad of the food they would creep up and get it. They allowed me nearer and nearer over the next couple of months. It was very satisfying to be gaining their trust!

I drove twenty miles one lunch break to collect some old wooden tea chests, which I talked a company into donating to me, for the cat's winter shelter. This was September and I knew the cold was coming. I also called Cat's Protection and a kind lady, called Kath, started getting me food for the colony. I didn't know CP existed until then! She started trapping the cats to get them "snipped" and checked for FIV etc. There were only females, except for the original old chap. I had never heard of FIV until then! When I look back at this now, some 8 years on I realise how much I have learned since!

I fed the colony seven days a week, twice a day. It relieved my job stress, but added it's own, as I felt so responsible for them and so in love with all these creatures. I had named them and then…one Sunday morning there was a young ginger trying to reach one of the dishes of food. Almost as one, the others turned and stared at him and everyone froze. I sensed trouble. I rushed in and grabbed the ginger and quite literally threw him into the car! I jumped in and he banged his head on the windscreen and the side windows a couple of times in his panic to escape. I turned on the engine and immediately he settled down on the front seat – I don't know what I would have done otherwise!

I drove home and from the driveway I called for my Husband to open all the doors so I could run into the utility room. For probably the only time in his life, my Husband didn't question what I said! I grabbed the ginger and ran. Well, I need not have worried! I put him on the counter

by the food dishes of my other cats, he sniffed, jumped down into the old dog bed, lay down for a minute, jumped back to the food and he was home! We never looked back…

He was about 9 months old and passed his vet check! Here is "Ginger" (really imaginative on my part) the first time he experienced sleeping on the back of a settee. You can image what happened next – yes, he slid all the way down fast asleep and had a rude awakening when he hit the seat!

I think he owes his life to some men in the local plumbing shop warehouse who set up a pipe for him to shelter in and gave him milk when he was very little. I asked around the area and nobody claimed him so he stayed!

You will come across him again in the "Green and Ginger Don't Mix" chapter – he has been a love since day one.

The next thing that happened at The Courthouse was that one of the men there complained to the Landlords about the cats and word came back that they had to go. I was terrified that these "suits" would do something to hurt the cats (like poison) if they didn't go, so reluctantly I used my contact with the RSPCA and they were trapped and removed. They were very depressed in the RSPCA cattery and I used to sit with them, but could not argue that they were unhappy and needed to be re-located. They went off to an animal sanctuary somewhere in Essex, I think. I was profoundly sad at having to say "goodbye". I also felt that I was the one person who had spent time building up their trust in people and had let them down because I could not take care of them. It taught me that I am certainly not fit to be a foster mother for CP as the pain of letting them go was horrendous even though I knew it was best for them.

I moved offices shortly thereafter. I had to leave the original old cat there and feel very bad that I abandoned him. I believe the other women went on feeding him "on the quiet"!

I had taken home one more cat when this colony was broken up and that was Sooty.

Sooty's Sanctuary

Sooty was all black, but his coat was dull as if coated in soot from a fire. I soon discovered that it was because he wasn't well…when I got him home and to the Vet he was diagnosed FIV. I didn't want to let him go too, so I quickly had an outdoor pen attached to my garden shed for him to live there and have a big area to play in. That was 1998 and the common practice then was to put FIV cats to sleep immediately. I couldn't and I did lots of internet research and found some could live. I fed him and brushed him and gave him vitamin E oil in his food and he started to look better and his coat glowed. He had been someone's pet at sometime in the dim and distant past as he was always able to be handled and used to curl up in my lap quite happily.

His downfall was my responsibility – my ignorance back then. Ginger used to come to the side of the pen and look in and Sooty would get really worked up and throw himself onto the wire covered walls – bit like a splatted cat! One day he did it on the door and my feeble catch burst open with the force of his weight. The next minute he was out, with me in hot pursuit, as I had been in the pen with him. After Ginger he went and there were lots of screams on both sides and a rough and tumble and Sooty looked intent on murder. When I finally got hold of him I felt that I couldn't take such a chance again – not only with my other cats but with the neighbours'. I hardened my heart and took him to be put to sleep immediately. I was ignorant and scared because of the FIV diagnosis.

It's been pointed out to me since, that because he had been defending his territory – a response to him having had to fight to survive when he'd been living rough - his instincts would have made him defensive of his food and security. It's an example of why each cat diagnosed with FIV needs to be looked at as an individual.

When Sooty died in my arms I promised him I would found a sanctuary in his memory – guilt on my part really. It has taken me years to accept that I alone cannot physically, financially or emotionally do it. The money from this book will go to help other cats. That is as much as I can do and purchasing Harry products means that you can help me to help them! See order form at back!

Teggy from Lanzarote

When my husband and I were on holiday in Lanzarote in 2003 we walked from our apartment down a path to the beach. On the way I noticed a cat sitting on the doorstep of a bungalow, facing the door as if asking to go in. She turned and looked at me and because of her look and her unusual markings I was a bit taken aback. I just "knew" that she would come and find me.

Yes, later that day she appeared at the bottom of the steps up to our apartment, quite a way from where I'd first seen her! Of course, I broke all the rules posted around the site by the property manager – I called her in and fed her what I had for my husband's supper!

No problem, there were shops just across the road. I did only buy human food there as I was afraid I would be seen buying cat food and then be in trouble! I went into the large town for the cat food!

It wasn't just that I didn't want to get into trouble. I didn't want Teggy in trouble. She was obviously used to surviving from one kindly holiday maker to another!

Teggy (because we were in Costa Teguese) soon became a regular visitor. She appeared every time we came home and surreptitiously she crept in for her food. During our holiday she became plump and her fur glossy.

It broke my heart to leave her there. I seriously contemplated bringing her to the UK. Apart from her having to share with my five other cats and two dogs and the trauma of flying, I wasn't sure she'd appreciate a cold and wet January! Every night ever since leaving her, I have prayed to God and her Guardian Angels to watch over her. I just hope they are doing a good job!

I contemplated going back the next winter, but decided it would be worse if I couldn't find her again. Like so many creatures I have seen when abroad, I am disgusted at the way they are treated in many countries. There must be hundreds of Teggies I just don't know about!

Tira the Norwegian Speaker!

Late one evening someone I knew (who knew I loved cats) knocked at the door and asked me to take in his fifteen year old tabby cat. He was in the middle of a divorce and the house was to be sold and the pets to be divided. There was no place for this elegant old lady. Well, the photo is not such an elegant pose, but very much how she liked to spend her time in the last two years of her life in our home!

![Tira the tabby cat lying on her back on the carpet in front of a radiator]

Tira's original human "mother" spoke Norwegian and I am sure that was Tira's preferred language as it was what she grew up with – you had to pronounce her name with that accent or she would not acknowledge you! She will be most remembered for standing in front of the fridge door and making a special commanding meow! Milk it had to be – small amount several times a day. Cat milk was ignored!

A Story from "Auntie" Rose

I had my own cat called Sam. Every summer a black feral tom cat came, and I fed him and gave him milk. He disappeared again every winter. This went on for years. When he did appear in the garden he would do a long "meow" which sounded like "Rose" to me! Was he really calling my name?

One day a friend was with me and said *"Someone is calling you."* I said *"It's the stray cat."* My friend was certain someone was calling my name until I took her into the garden and showed her the cat.

Then one summer, he turned up as usual in the garden, but I could see something was wrong. I put food and milk out, but he couldn't seem to eat. No one could get close to him and where he lay in the sun the flies started to crawl on him and he didn't bother.

I phoned the RSPCA. They would not do anything unless I caught him myself which I explained I could not do.

A lady from Cats Protection brought a cage to my garden to trap him in and we set it up with milk. I watched for a couple of hours and eventually he went in for a drink and we got him!

When I saw him up close his mouth was a mess. The Cats Protection lady came to collect him and took him to the vet. I asked her to let me know what happened to him. She phoned and told me he had cancer and had been put to sleep straight away to ease his suffering.

I have always felt he came to me because he knew one day he would need my help. I shed many a tear over him. Still, I feel honoured that he came into my life.

I never had a name for him when he was alive, now I think he should be known as "Gruffalo". It's the name of a children's story monster that was very scary, but also soft on the inside. Sounds perfect to me!

Lyra and the Pens!

A quirky obsession is how my friend Clare described her cat's love of pens! I bet there are other pen lovers out in the world too!

Lyra loves pens. They can disappear anywhere in the house. Lyra seeks them out. She is happy to upset pen holders, take them off tables, etc.

She then rolls them to her mat in the kitchen and puts them underneath! A secret hideaway no less!

Now, when Clare wants a pen she just looks under her mat! There are usually half a dozen there!

If you have a cat with quirky habits and would like their story included on Harry's website please email the story to:

susanjane.smith@btconnect.com

Thomas

This is a story from "Auntie Janet". My cats have lots of "Aunties" because most of my friends have cats…correction all of my friends have cats now or have had them in the past. I do not want to be around people who don't love them! Anyway, I knew Thomas for many years and I will always believe he chose to come to Janet and Danny (he's soft too) because he knew he would find love and care. Thomas would never have survived without them. This is Janet's story:-

"He arrived in our garden looking very forlorn and wary, keeping his distance. Eventually hunger got the better of him and he ventured over from his favoured spot underneath the conifers to investigate the dish, which I had offered. Having retreated into the kitchen and closed the door, I watched from behind net curtains in another room from where I could also get a closer look at him. He was a rather sorry sight. He was very thin with a very dull coat, and there seemed to be a problem with his eyes. I watched as he tried desperately to eat. Obviously very hungry he appeared to be acting very strangely as he backed away from the offered food, hissing and 'pawing' at it. This behaviour continued over a period of a few weeks while, at the same time, he was getting used to me. The weather grew colder and so I began to leave the kitchen door open a little, and eventually in he came and settled under a radiator. We called him Thomas and he took to being stroked and gently spoken to.

When I felt he had sufficient confidence in me, I popped him in a cat basket and off to the Vet we went. His age was guessed at about four years. According to the Vet he had contracted conjunctivitis as a kitten, which had been neglected. This gave the impression of cataracts. It was felt he saw as though looking through smoky glass. The bottom eyelashes were also growing inwards which made them weep with pus. The latter issue was dealt with through a minor operation.

His odd eating habit was due to a mouth virus, which we attempted to keep under control with permanent antibiotics over several years. After considerable veterinary care and a change of Vet in the practice that was younger and more knowledgeable on the mouth problem, she suggested a couple of minor operations, which included the removal of several teeth. With continued tender loving care and the much-improved diet, his health improved greatly, and we were able to dispense with the antibiotics. His lovely black and white coat shone. The virus in his mouth fell dormant, and he became a much-loved pet.

His addition to our family of three female cats proved to be an eye opener in the hierarchy of the cat world. The older female cat was queen inside the house, and he deferred to the other two females - after all they were all here first, but outside he was definitely king. He used to patrol, with authority, the perimeter of our large garden often standing 'on sentry duty' at the front of the house. He was invariably at this post to give his friendly greeting on my return home. There was always the odd skirmish indoors if he attempted to get his food without adhering to the established pecking order.

Thomas had an additional fourteen years of life in a loving environment following his arrival in our garden as eventually his mouth condition would have confined him to slow starvation. His poor eyesight was compensated by extra fine hearing, smell and sensing.

It was with great sadness that we had to end his life last year (2005) as his kidneys were failing and nothing was alleviating this failure. He had become completely blind too."

Janet's modesty forbids her to say that the quality of life Thomas achieved was due in large part to her open purse, hours of care and lots of love. He found the best home any cat could have with Janet and, of course, Danny!

The Sugar Plum Fairy
This is his cute pose!

Sugar is short for this longer name. He got his name because he was such a sweet kitten. He was a kitten who used to knock my milk bottle over and he still loves milk!

He used to pop in my door every chance he got and eat the other cats' food. Then I started letting him curl up and sleep – his choice really.

Unexpectedly, one day, the man of the couple where Sugar lived banged on my door and was shouting and swearing and before I could open the door he had head butted it on the glass pane – it was a wonder it didn't break his skin or my glass! I would have given him the cat but by then I was too scared to open the door…I lived alone (except for two dogs and the 3 cats). Next thing a policeman knocked and said he had to take the cat. So I waved Sugar "goodbye".

Thereafter, whenever I took my dogs out for a walk that man used to come out with Sugar (still only about 6 months old) in his hand and hold him high in the air and squeeze his tummy until he cried out in pain. I didn't dare respond as I was sure that was what he wanted me to do. I later learned he really was a nasty piece of work in other ways and ended up in prison.

It used to tear me apart to hear that young creature in such pain. I decided I would do something about it and I contacted a lady in the local Cats Protection. I didn't tell her the full story as I was afraid she would not be able to help if I did. I knew nothing about the work of CP or the RSPCA back then having just come over from living in the USA.

When I was getting ready to move house and leave the area I decided I couldn't leave Sugar there. After dark one night I saw Sugar looking for milk and I opened the door and in he walked. I popped him into a large, zipper bag and walked out to the car with him. I think he knew what I was trying to do because he didn't make a sound!

Off I rushed and took him to some friends ten miles away – as cat lovers they were willing accomplices! He stayed with them that night and the next day I took him to the Vet who cut off the mats of fur and "snipped" his fathering potential. He went back to my friends for rest and recovery and then on to the CP lady. There he stayed for five weeks and I went to see him every day. No one claimed him even though CP advertised him.

When I was settled in my new home he came to live with me. I lived in fear for six years that the man would find us. Six years was the time the police had told me that he had to be with me to be legally mine. We made it! Sugar is now a very elderly gent of sixteen. Just as sweet as ever. It felt like I had risked my life for him – no regrets. He was worth the effort.

What a Difference a Year Makes

By Cover Girl Smith
(Holly made the front cover of the local CP newsletter!)

In cat terms a year may not seem like a long time – this last one has been life changing for me. My name is Holly and about a year ago Jackie from The Forest of Dean Branch of Cats Protection kindly snatched me from a bed and I kindly drew blood because I didn't know what lay ahead. I had a hard life and had been hurt physically and mentally, including losing a hind leg due to a person's cruelty. Enough of that!

After meeting Sara (another CP lady) I met a funny person called Sue who loved me the minute she saw me. I was not much to look at as I could only drag myself around on my remaining three legs. I growled at everyone including my son, Charlie, whom I didn't like any better than anyone else. I went to stay with Sue, initially in a kitten pen, because I couldn't mix with her four other cats. Nor, frankly, would I have wanted to do so!

The first morning Richard, my new Daddy, opened the pen and scooped me up. He turned me on my back in his arms and tickled my tummy! Well, what a way to treat any cat, let alone someone who was grumpy. I loved it and him immediately and purred for him – just a little, you understand.

Sue gave me several hours of Reiki healing every day and I was too 'limp' to bother objecting. She also played a string game with me and introduced me to a ball. Slowly, very slowly, I started to think my life was getting better. I had food on tap all day long and lots of love. After a couple of weeks I was allowed to try out my new garden under Mum's supervision. My new Mummy cried as I dragged my way up the steep slope. Still, it was lovely to be out in the fresh air and sunshine.

Lots more Reiki and then an introduction to the other animals of the house. Two huge border collies and the other cats. Well, I decided attack was the best form of defence and I was a horror to all of them. I still boss them all and they all let me be top cat and that includes those dogs! What patience they all had with me. Nobody hit back and eventually I decided to stop growling – took several months though!

Now I can WALK on all three legs and I can even run that way sometimes. Scooting on my bum is best when nervous.

Not that I have any worries these days. My cat sitters called me "Little Madam" because I am so bossy. I call when I'm outside or somewhere in the house and can't see any of my people. I also lie on the white cloth on the dining room table and have treats from my Daddy's plate. I've tasted all the human food I can. My favourite is a string of spaghetti held overhead so that I can lay on my back and slowly munch it into my mouth…such fun and yummy too.

Now I'm just coming in from a lovely stroll around the garden and a nap under my favourite shrub. I have a full tummy and life is good. What a difference the year has made to my life…why not make such a difference to someone else's life?

There is usually enough room in your heart to squeeze another little one in! Please call your local animal rescue centre today!

PS

I find it's impossible to catch dragonflies when you have only one hind leg. I leap about, but…

Do you have any suggestions?

COMPLEMENTARY THERAPY FOR CATS

I am a Psychotherapist with over 20 years of experience and much of that has been working with people who have been victims of child abuse and other traumas. In the course of helping people to learn to overcome their experiences I have looked into various complementary therapeutic approaches. I use "complementary" rather than talk in terms of "alternative" therapy as I consider that it is important to work with GP's and in the case of animals, Vets! I would never recommend that anyone not use the medical facilities that they offer.

Personally, I have had traumatised and rescue animals for years and I have had the privilege of giving Reiki Healing at a branch of the RSPCA and a branch of Cats Protection so have seen a wide variety of cats. Here is some information about treatments that you might want to consider discussing with your Vet:

Reiki

This Japanese word is understood to mean Universal Life Energy. It originates from ancient Hindu/Buddhist teachings and has been passed down via Reiki Masters. When a Reiki Practioner provides a treatment to an animal the pet will probably experience a pleasant sensation of warmth or gentle tingling. The Energy is coming through the therapist's hands and stimulates the pet's energy to help it release stress and tension and come into balance. Reiki facilitates a sense of deep relaxation and increases feelings of wellbeing in people and I believe it does the same for animals. This in turn activates the body's natural ability to heal itself.

I have had the privilege of giving Reiki healing to a wide variety of animals and I especially love seeing some cats come to me and "ask" for my hands to be placed upon them. It is also possible for the healing energy to be sent "long distance" but that is not something I enjoy as much as touching fur! I have worked in this way with toads, various insects, a horse, dogs, wild birds and a mouse. It's very interesting to experience and I would encourage any pet owner to go on a Reiki course to learn how to do it for their own animals.

Bach Flower Remedies

Do read "Bach Flower Remedies for Animals" by S.Ball and J.Howard (ISBN 0 85207 296 1) and do check with your Vet. It is my understanding that these remedies can be given to animals – four drops of the DILUTED Mixture four times a day. **Not to be given to a pregnant or lactating animal.**

My experience is that not only is it useful to use Rescue Remedy, but also Mimulus is excellent for reducing fear and thus the lashing out that can occur when a cat is anxious.

Bioforce

This company's products are flower essences and there again should not be given without talking to your Vet and **not when an animal is pregnant or lactating.**

Their liquid Echinacea for humans, Bioforce say, may be used to boost the immune system in animals, so do get your Vet to check this out!

Healing Angels

I frequently use creative visualization with my psychotherapy clients including the Angel Exercises of Diana Cooper from her book: *"A Little Light on Angels"*. The imagery seems to work for people so I see no harm in asking Healing Angels and Guardian Angels to help with animal problems. Go to the Vet also, though!

The theory is that the Angels will come, but you do have to ask!

Personally, I also believe in the power of prayer!

GREEN AND GINGER DO NOT MIX

By Holly Smith

Well, now that I can walk says Holly; I have started looking around at my brothers and sisters in the household. This includes a large, handsome ginger cat, called Ginger! He started life as a feral kitten so has a tipped ear but, apart from that he is lovely and very patient with me, much to everyone's surprise!

The other day, my new Mum was staining the garden bench a rather smart shade of green and Ginger thought that spreading the droplets would be a great help to her. Not impressed with the results she put him under the tap to get the large green splodge off his back. Rubbing up against the furniture can be a bit dodgy! Then came the beautifully decorated ear totally covered in this Cuprinol stain. It wiped off easily as it was not yet set.

To add insult to injury the stain was called "Holly" colour. Don't know why they didn't get my permission first! Luckily all is now well and Ginger is nothing but ginger, such a great winter spice!

This is Ginger on the table that ended up Holly green along with him!

Gus, Auntie Christine and the Others

Holly loved my friend Christine from the moment they met and that was mutual! Chris was in my office interviewing me and Holly (because she had spent her recovery time in my office in a kitten pen) was at the door asking to come in. At that stage she still didn't walk and dragged herself over to Chris who lifted Holly up gently and cuddles ensued. Holly re-awakened in Christine her love of cats and so Hector found a home. I should say Major General Sir Hector Warwick! Hector says that naturally he is the cat sitting on the chair! The other is Gus.

Chris has shared these anecdotes for your edification!

Gus

Christine says "let me tell you a cat story which I hope will make you smile…The cat with whom I had the longest relationship was very special. He was called Gus, and he died in 2000 aged 17. In fact my relationship with Gus lasted longer than that with either of my husbands, so I am sure you understand what I mean! Gus died when I was away on business. My friends buried him in the garden and put up a wooden cross for him, as he was undoubtedly a Christian cat.

Anyway, I missed him desperately, especially as he had been such a character and a loving companion. I decided to have a memorial stone erected in his memory. This was engraved with the words:

"Gus 1983 - 2000. A Very Fine Cat"

The stone was put in place, and as I was admiring it and thinking of Gus, it occurred to me for the first time, that I had not had a memorial stone erected for my Father when he died in 1996. I felt dreadful. I could not believe that I had thought to do it for Gus, but not for my own Father!

I mentioned my shame to a friend of mine. After thinking for a few seconds, she said, *"Well, I wouldn't worry, because after all, your Father wasn't very religious."* My response was, *"Well I don't suppose Gus was, either."* To which she replied: *"You never know. I am sure he was saying prayers every time he waited to be fed!"*

Ginger and Algy

Christine says these were two ginger litter twins, handsome boys, but very naughty. Ginger was so-called because he was, er, ginger and Algy

because 'Ginger and Algy' were a pair of chums of the fictional character Capt. Biggles.

In the early 1990's, not long after the fall of the Berlin Wall, I was living and working in Bratislava, the capital of Slovakia. Ginger and Algy were back home in Wales, cared for by a friend in my absence.

During one particular week, this friend was absent, and a neighbour had stepped into the breach. But I needed to access the messages on my home answer phone – and in those days telephone technology was not sufficiently advanced to enable you to pick them up remotely from abroad, although you could do so from within the UK. So I asked another friend to do just that – and arranged to 'phone her so she could tell me what the messages were.

But Ginger and Algy had other ideas…They chewed through the answer phone cable, completely ruining the machine and thwarting my plans. I phoned my friend from my flat in Bratislava to tell her, opening the conversation with the words, "Ginger and Algy have severed international communications…" There were lots of clicks and other unfamiliar noises on the line, but we continued our chat.

It was only later that I learned that, in those post-soviet times, as a foreigner my phone was almost certainly tapped by the Slovak security services – a case, apparently, of old habits dying hard. But I have often wondered since if the names 'Ginger and Algy' are on some list of suspected secret agents! Maybe someone somewhere is still looking for them!

My Beautiful Beauty

Sadly I had to put her to sleep this Spring 2006 because her kidneys were failing. The Vet had done a wonderful job and gave her three extra years with medicine for low thyroid. She used to lay on her back in my Husband's arms for her medicine very willingly for the majority of the time and then one day I realised that she had started to fight having the medicine. It was time. I dug her grave in the garden and bought a beautiful pink azalea to put on the top. I sobbed all the while. Usually I have had my cats cremated and then brought the ashes to other gardens where I have lived.

I felt I should bury Beauty. I speak to her every day as I pass and she was truly pretty when in flower. We've put stones around the base of the plant not only to stop the fox digging, but to remind me not to move that shrub!

My tribute to her I did in the form of the column I wrote for the local newspaper on a weekly basis. Here it is in case it is of help to anyone you come across:

Question: I am heartbroken. I recently had my cat put to sleep because she was old and ill. People tell me *"It was only a cat",* but she was my companion for over fifteen years. Why am I so upset?

Answer: Jenny de Vries in *"Cat Quotations"* (published by Exley) says "To some blind souls all cats are much alike. To a cat lover every cat from the beginning of time has been utterly and amazingly unique". Cats (and dogs) give people unconditional love – a rare quality to receive! It would be unreasonable if you didn't miss your cat terribly. This is grief – just like when a human dies – and it hurts. You can feel not only lonely, but despairing of life ever feeling better.

What is worse in many pet deaths is that you, as a responsible owner, have to make decisions on your pet's behalf. They cannot tell you what they want. When you take a decision to end a life it is not a choice that you would normally be called upon to make. You have to make a decision about what is in the best interest of the animal concerned, regardless of how distressing it is for you to lose that beloved creature. This makes the responsibility and the loss even greater and more painful.

You might try talking to the Pet Bereavement Support Service on 0800 096 6606. They have telephone befrienders who can provide compassion. The Society for Companion Animal Studies can provide a leaflet if you contact them at 10b Leny Road, Callander FK17 8BA. You might also find it useful to read *"Goodbye, Dear Friend"* by Virginia Ironside (published by Robson).

In my opinion, departed cats are very happy when we take in another bundle of fur that needs a home, so you might like to contact your local animal rescue centre. My experience is that it will take the edge off your pain when you have another cat to nurture!

Harry and Telepathy

To sleep in safety is such bliss!

"Harry's Home!" This is what we say whenever he strolls in the house. I'm so grateful that he has returned because his new sister, Holly (of three legged fame in a previous story) has been horrible to him – hissing and chasing. Holly scoots on her bum like she used to do before she could walk on her third leg. She is as quick as lightning and poor Harry runs for his life until he climbs up a tree, trellis or fence!

Now, Harry is around 5 years old and bigger and stronger than little Holly. Still he is the one who runs! He is normally very self possessed and quite capable of patting the dog, Duke, on the nose if the dog steps out of line. I'd love to know what goes on in their minds!

To that end I tried some telepathy on him! Now, you may be thinking that I have lost my mind, but I swear that he told me his name was "Harry" and not "Manny" as Cats Protection had down as being his name. Harry also "told" me his Mummy was looking for him and that her name was Tiddles. He "showed" me a picture of her from when he was suckling her: white body with black tail and black on shoulders! It was a side-on image and I am sure I didn't just make it up!

By the way, he would still like us to find his Mum so if you have ever known such a female, perhaps from the Tutnals area of Lydney, Gloucestershire do let me know!

Back to the telepathy! I have always wanted to be Dr. Doolittle and talk to the animals. This all really started when I was lent a book called *"Cat Talk"* by Sonya Fitzpatrick. That led me on to reading her book "What the Animals Tell Me". Wonderful animal stories even for the sceptics! I just think she is plausible. Particularly see her page on what to do!

Here's what I did for you to try: Make yourself very relaxed (meditation, deep breathing, whatever technique that works for you). Ask the animal's permission to communicate as it is important to be respectful. Also, the animal does need to be willing and you do need their attention. It is pointless trying when a cat is watching a bird, etc. Silently say the animal's name in your mind. Imagine your pet's appearance as you are saying its name and send out a "picture" of its body along with its name. Ask it to come to you. Ask it specific, simple questions and see if you get an answer! The answers may come in the form of an image rather than words – you have to learn to connect in their language not ours. If this happens you have connected telepathically.

This is all done using the power of your mind - when you are still and silent. Do read Sonya's work. It would be wonderful if we really could talk to the animals and they could "tell" us where they hurt and what they want! It has the potential to bring joy to all of us – humans and animals alike!

In Memory of Happy

Original Author Unknown. This was given to me when my old, faithful dog, Happy died. I think it stands the test of time and can just as easily be adapted to think about a cat.

If It Should Be

If it be I grow old and weak
And pain should wake me from my sleep
Then you must do what must be done
For this last battle can't be won
You will be sad I understand
Don't let your grief then stay your hand
For this day more than all the rest
Your love and friendship stand the test.

We've had so many happy years
What is to come will hold no fears
You'll not want me to suffer
So when the time comes, please let me go
I know in time you will see
It is kindness you do to me

Although my tail it's last has waved
From pain and suffering I've been saved
Do not grieve that it should be you
Who has to decide this thing to do
We've been so close, we two, these years
Don't let your heart hold any tears.

Ode to Sweetie

I had the privilege of burying Sweetie in my garden. I had met this sweet old lady when The Forest of Dean Branch of Cats Protection took her into care: blind, deaf, starving and wandering the streets. Wandering? No, crawling along the wall for guidance. Torties have a bit of a reputation. Not so Sweetie! Someone must have loved her once. She loved the cuddles she got from Carol (her foster Mum).

Sad as this story is, at least for the last month of her life Sweetie knew she was loved, kept warm and fed. She also got as much treatment as the Vet could provide. When the final decision was made, it was quite simply to stop the pain she was suffering that night. Afterwards it was beautiful to see her at peace. Carol and I gave her the best funeral we could, including this poem I wrote especially for her:

Ode to Sweetie
Life is energy, it cannot be destroyed
The psychics say
You are spiritual beings
Who pass this way.

We've released you from your body of pain
To go to the other "plain"
Where joy abounds
And happiness reigns

Where care and worries
Fade to bliss
You were much loved
You will be missed.

You have healing paws
An angel now
God bless.

About the Author

Pure bliss is what I experience when I sit with a cat and it purrs. They are the best moments in my life and always have been. The only thing to beat it is handling kittens which I sometimes get the privilege of doing for Cats Protection – they need socializing when young for the best chance of being homed.

When I do Reiki Healing on an animal and it starts to trust and relax it's a joy. I've been so lucky.

Professionally, I'm a Psychotherapist in private practice since 1987 and spend my working days creating emotional health for people. My private life is shared with five rescue cats and two rescue Border Collies, and a Husband, but he knows his place! Our household is a demonstration that cats and dogs can live together in peace!

Other Books by the Same Author

"Pre-Marital MOT: A Relationship Inspection"
Published by Counselling in the Forest
See **www.counsellingintheforest.co.uk**

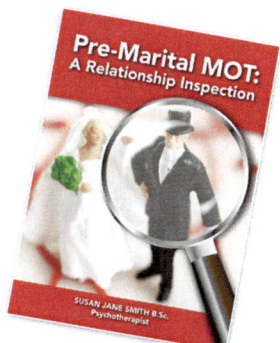

"Emotional Health for Emotional Wealth"
ISBN 0-9553698-2-7
      978-0-9553698-2-7

Harry's Home Order Form

£1 from each purchase helps to support cat rescue work - YOU CHOOSE!

☐ FOD Cats Protection **OR** ☐ Please specify _____

Description	Price	Sizes	Qty	State Colour/s	Sub Total
BOOK "Harry's Home – A Cat Compendium"	£9.99			n/a	
CHOCOLATE HARRY'S Handmade & delicious!	£9.99				
T-SHIRT – with embroidered logo Colours: Azalea Pink, Iris, Jade Green Please note: Chest size is actual width of material	£9.99	Small (36") Medium (40") Large (44") X Large (48") XX Large (52")			
POLO SHIRT – with embroidered logo Colours: Royal Blue, Bright Red, Green *Please note: Chest size is actual width of material* Children's shirts by special order	£13.99	Small (36") Medium (40") Large (44") X Large (48") XX Large (52")			
				Order Value:	
Only pre-paid orders can be accepted!			Postage & Packaging:		£4.50
				Donation:	
Please make cheques payable to: **Sue Smith** Tel: 01594 564308				Total Due:	

Please make cheques payable to: **Sue Smith**
Tel: 01594 564308

Post your order form and cheque to:
P O Box 78, Yorkley, Lydney, Gloucestershire, GL15 4WT, England

Your Contact Details and Delivery Address:

Name: _____

Tel No: _____ Email: _____

Address: _____

_____

Town: _____ County/State: _____

Post/Zip Code: _____ Country: _____

Please allow 28 days for delivery — **Thank you for your support, it's really appreciated!**

The Cacao Tree

·C H O C O L A T I E R S·

Proud makers of deliciously milky Chocolate Harrys in support of cat rescue charities

The Cacao Tree uses high quality Belgian 'converture' chocolate with high levels of cocoa solids to create an extensive range of delicious chocolate.
Our recipes are original and we include Fairtrade and Organic products in our range.

www.thecacaotree.co.uk

Taurus Crafts, Lydney, Gloucestershire GL15 6BU
Tel: Clare Shepherd 01600 716735